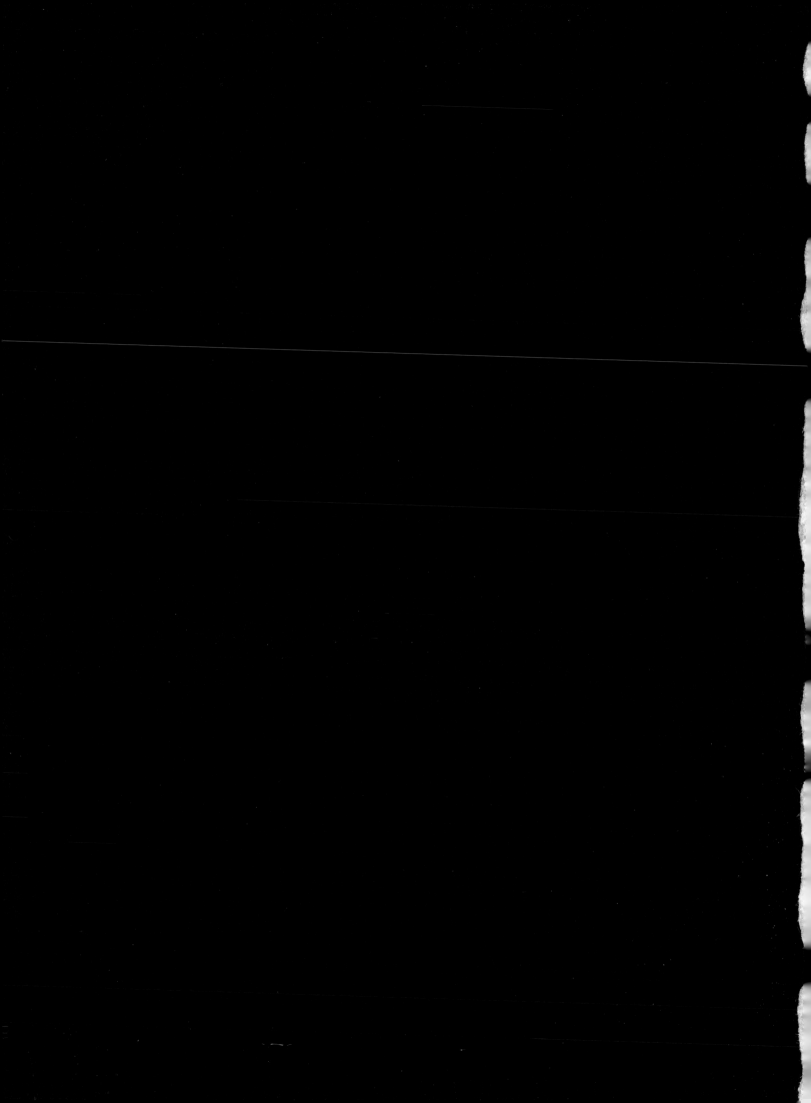

English Rose

Byron Newman

COLLECTOR'S EDITIONS, LTD.

The author wishes to thank the following people for their kind support and collaboration with the production of this book: REMY HADDAD and PATRICK ROBIN, DANIEL FILIPACCHI, JEAN DEMACHY, REGIS PAGNIEZ, FRANCIS DUMOULIN and all the staff of LUI, BRIAN WRAY and IMPERIAL TOBACCO PLC, MARK RAMAGE and JOHN PETERS of SHARPS ADVERTISING, RALPH GELLERT of PERMANITE LTD, MARIANNE and CLAUDE AVICE (PARIS), ARNE HASSELQVIST (MUSTIQUE), SIMON HOWARD, FRANCIS FULFORD SEBASTIAN FENWICK, ANDRE BERCOFF, CAROLINE HAMILTON-FLEMING, PERCIVAL SAVAGE, MARTIN SINOTT, PETER FULLER, HERBIE SCHNEIDER, ADRIAN KNOWLES, CHRIS WORLEY and JACQUES TRINQUART.

He would also like to thank the following designers and shops who kindly helped him 'undress' his models: BRADLEY'S OF KNIGHTSBRIDGE for lingerie, MANOLO BLAHNIK and CHARLES JOURDAN for shoes, ANTONY PRICE, BASTET, PHILIP HOCKLEY, QUASIMODO, PHILIP SOMERVILLE and HERBERT JOHNSON.

The author also thank his assistants: JONATHON PILKINGTON and HAMISH MITCHELL-COTTS, and the make-up artists and hairdressers who have worked on the photographic sessions, in particular: PATTI BURRIS and BASTIAN.

Finally, special thanks to all the models who have accepted to appear in this book, and particularly to LINZI DREW, GLORIA DOUSE, CAROLINE HALLETT, ANDREA KOVIK and TONI WHITE and to SAM and MIKE from SAMANTHA BOND MANAGEMENT, MELISSA RICHARDSON and all the team at TAKE TWO MODEL AGENCY, NICK and VERONICA at CRAWFORDS, JOSEE and DICK at MODELS ONE and LARAINE ASHTON.

All the photographs in this book were styled by BRIGITTE ARIEL.

PREFACE

Dreams of beautiful women adrift in an old imperial mist – the pale girl whose eyes slant across a hushed landscape as she waits in torment for the beastly lover, or the rosy bride whose flesh would smash like porcelain were it not rendered both yielding and resistant by the tensile rigor of her ambition, or the dark exotic girl whom fate has drawn from faraway and imprisoned among the sublime and ghostly fetishes of an abandoned palace – constricted, lustful and caressing, elegant in repose, capricious in action, taking up and discarding masks in response to obscure impulses from the heart – sweet rather than bitter – where such harsh emotion might have been, there is instead an unexpected zigzag of cruelty which is bitterness made intelligent by desire – the libido, trapped behind a lattice of introspection, aggravated by restraint, seeks eccentric escape, springs wetly into the light – knowledgeable, but with the vanity of knowledge diffused through a subtle humor – an ancient liberty which confers poise and at the same time stimulates an inner restlessness and this gives the personality a tension, an edge – and warmth, perhaps also unexpected, because it is rarely flaunted but comes with intimacy – these notions of English eroticism which infest the general imagination slide into sharp focus in the photographs of Byron Newman. The act of sharpening shatters the cliché, destroys the symbol, and a specific event becomes, for a moment, possible.

Duncan Fallowell
London, february 1985

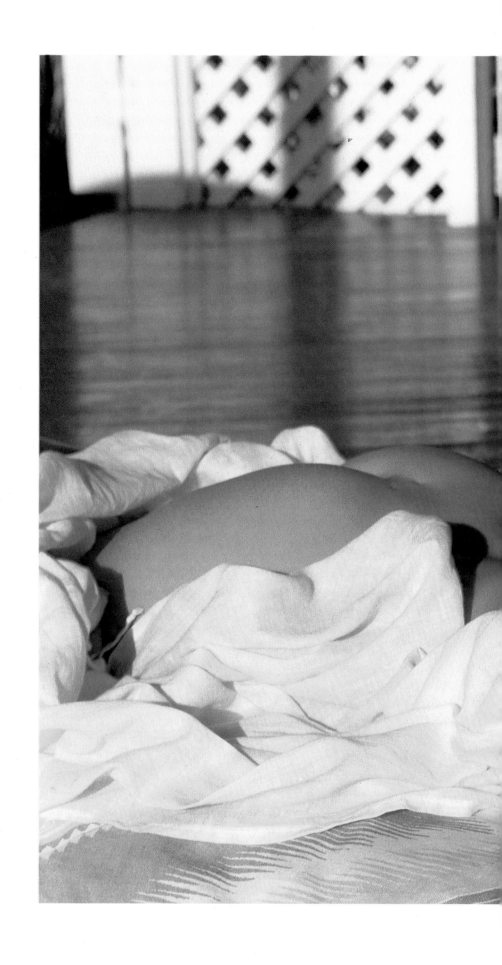

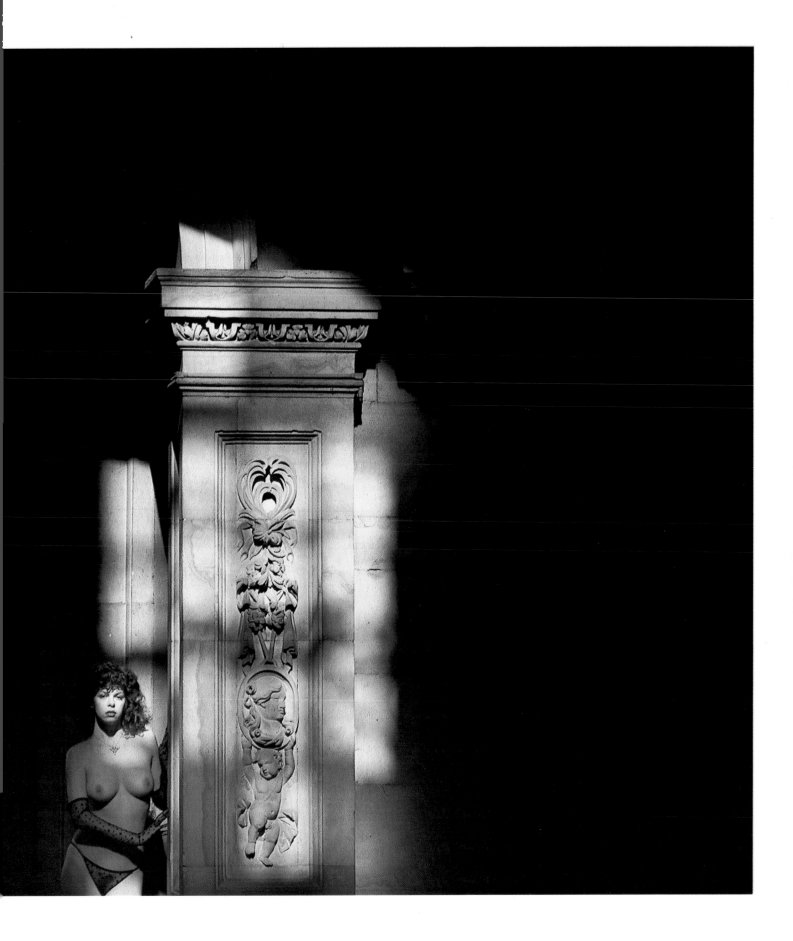

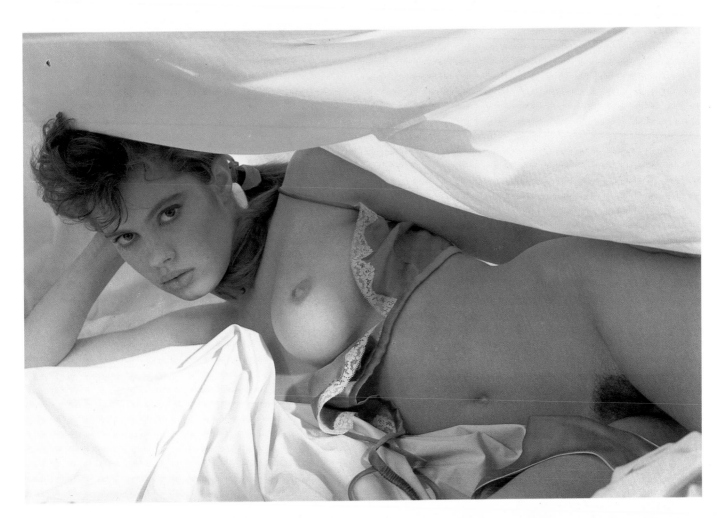

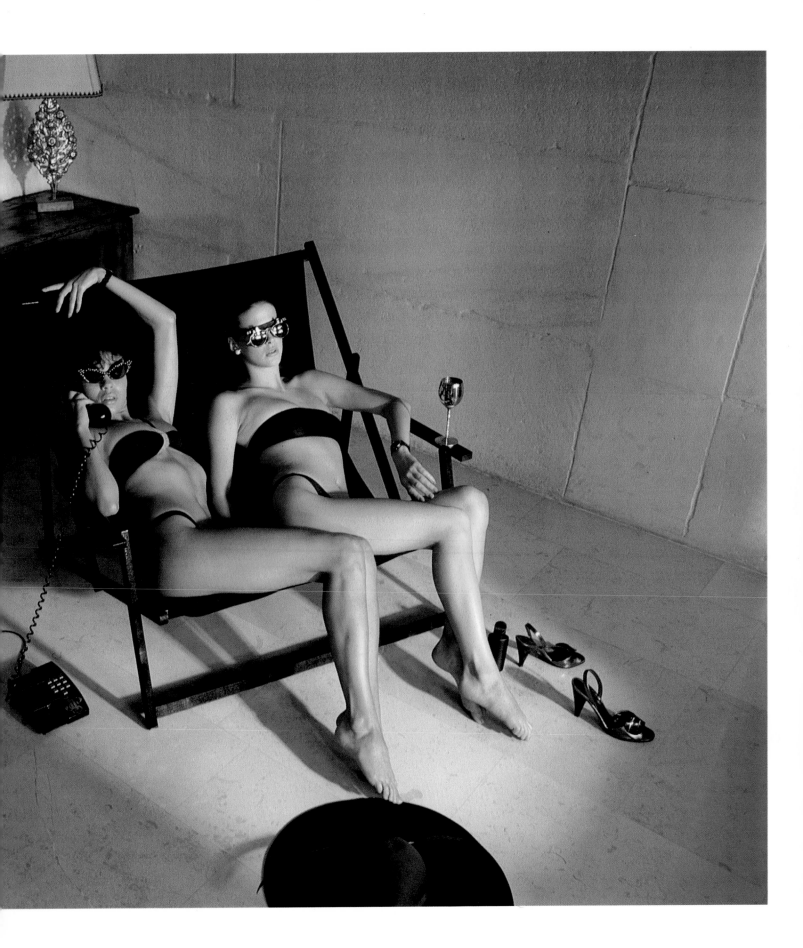